On the Waverley Route
Edinburgh-Carlisle in Colour

ROBERT ROBOTHAM

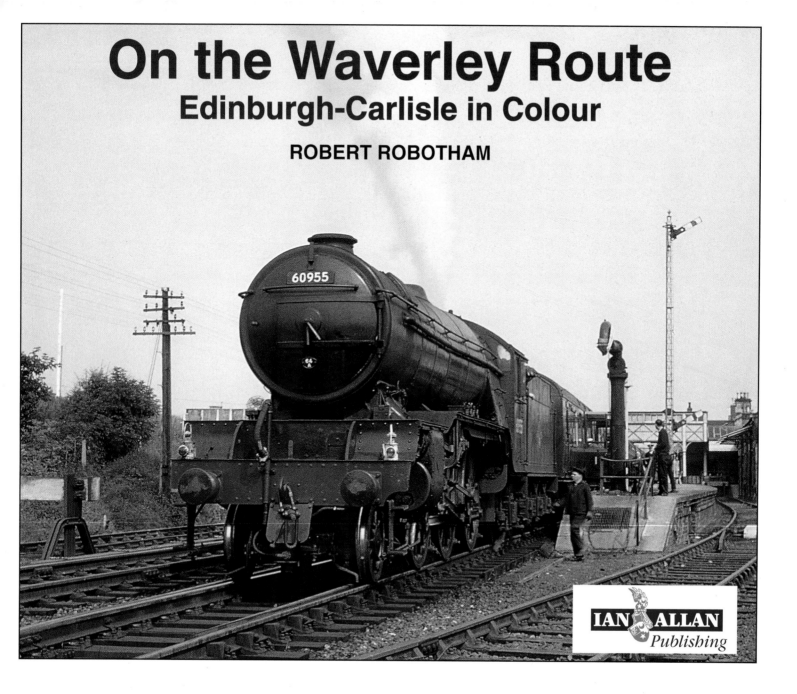

IAN ALLAN
Publishing

THE WAVERLEY

RESTAURANT CAR EXPRESS

LONDON (St. Pancras), SHEFFIELD (Midland)
LEEDS (City) and EDINBURGH (Waverley)

WEEKDAYS

		am					am
LONDON (St. Pancras)	dep	9 15	**EDINBURGH (Waverley)**	dep			10 15
NOTTINGHAM (Midland) {	arr	11 13	GALASHIELS	..	..	,,	11 5
	dep	11 17	MELROSE ..	..	..	,,	11 11
		pm	ST. BOSWELLS	..	..	,,	11 19
CHESTERFIELD (Midland) ..	dep	12 1	HAWICK	..	..	,,	11 35
SHEFFIELD (Midland) {	arr	12 18					pm
	dep	12 23	NEWCASTLETON ..	..	,,		12 9
LEEDS (City) .. {	arr	1 26	CARLISLE ..	..	{	arr	12 43
	dep	1 32			{	dep	12 51
SKIPTON .. .. {	arr	2 4	APPLEBY (West) ..		{	arr	1 25
	dep	2 6			{	dep	1 26
HELLIFIELD .. .. {	arr	2 18	SETTLE ..	.. dep			2 12
	dep	2 21	HELLIFIELD	{	arr		2 21
SETTLE	dep	2 29		{	dep		2 23
APPLEBY (West) .. {	arr	3 16	SKIPTON	{	arr		2 35
	dep	3 21		{	dep		2 37
CARLISLE .. .. {	arr	3 51	LEEDS (City) ..	{	arr		3 8
	dep	3 58		{	dep		3 15
NEWCASTLETON ..	.. arr	4 33	ROTHERHAM (Masboro') ..	dep			4 18
HAWICK	.. ,,	5 7	SHEFFIELD (Midland)	{	arr		4 27
ST. BOSWELLS ..	.. ,,	5 27		{	dep		4 33
MELROSE ..	.. ,,	5 36	CHESTERFIELD (Midland) ..	arr			4 52
GALASHIELS ..	.. ,,	5 42	NOTTINGHAM (Midland) {	arr			5 35
EDINBURGH (Waverley)	,,	6 34		dep			5 41
			LONDON (St. Pancras)	arr			7 40

Seats are reservable in advance for passengers travelling from London (St. Pancras) and Edinburgh (Waverley) on payment of a fee of 2s. 0d. per seat.

Restaurant Car for Table d'Hôte meals.

Front cover: 'V2' No 60813 storms to Tynehead and Falahill with an up Waverley route freight in April 1965. These freights were inter regional workings from Edinburgh Millerhill to Carlisle Kingmoor yards both expanded under the British Railways modernisation plan. These yards soon became shadows of their former selves with the demise of the small wagon load business and the conversion to block train working. The climb up to Tynehead and Falahill was at 1 in 70 and commenced at Hardengreen Junction some 10 miles away. *T. B. Owen ColourRail (SC281)*

Back cover: BRCW Bo-Bo, (now Class 26), No D5316 enters Galashiels with the 14.45 local service from Edinburgh Waverley to Carlisle in October 1964. Diesels were regular Waverley route performers adding to the good variety of motive power used on the line. *G. Devine/ColourRail (DE1246)*

Left: Timetable for the 'Waverley' restaurant car express for the period 10 September 1962 to 16 June 1963.

Previous page: 'V2' No 60955 awaits departure from St Boswells with the 09.50 Edinburgh-Leeds service on 14 August 1965. The branch platform for Kelso can be seen on the right, unfortunately the goods shed seems to have been closed. *K. M. Falconer/Colour Rail (SC701)*

First published 1995

ISBN 0 7110 2414 6

© Ian Allan Ltd 1995

Designed by Alan C. Butcher

Published by Ian Allan Publishing

an imprint of Ian Allan Ltd, Terminal House, Station Approach, Shepperton, Surrey TW17 8AS; and printed by Ian Allan Printing Ltd, Coombelands House, Coombelands Lane, Addlestone, Weybridge, Surrey KT15 1HY.

Introduction

This book covers the last years of one of Britain's great railways. Running from Carlisle to Edinburgh through the English and Scottish border counties, the line was known to most as the 'Waverley Route', but to railwaymen as the 'Long Road'.

'What a line this was!' is often said about the 'Waverley' by all that knew it. Running through harsh and remote countryside, steam locomotives could be seen in spectacular surroundings as well as putting up exciting performances themselves. However, despite (certainly in the northern part,) linking important border towns, the whole route closed on 5 January 1969.

Like the Great Central and Somerset & Dorset there was no large national campaign such as the one that helped to save the Settle to Carlisle route in the 1980s. However, there was a vociferous local campaign which culminated with the last train, (the 9.55pm. 'Night Midlander' Edinburgh to St Pancras sleeper), on the 5 January 1969, being halted at Newcastleton level crossing for an hour due to the gates being padlocked by the minister and parishioners. The day before, the last BR organised special over the route was hauled by Class 47 No D1974 which witnessed banner-waving protesters at most of the stations. The following day at Riddings Junction a length of track was lifted in front of invited press reporters to formally truncate the route. Unfortunately, in the 1960s it seemed that road traffic was in an unstoppable ascendancy and that nothing could be done to save the railways. It is only comparatively recently that some reversal in the fortunes of rail has taken place, with many stations and some lines re-opening — indeed as I write this proposals have been submitted to re-open the Waverley route as far as Galashiels from Edinburgh.

The Waverley route was not built as a single entity. The North British Railway originally bought the Edinburgh & Dalkeith Railway, (at the time worked by horses!), which came complete with an extension authorised to Hawick, opening throughout in 1849. Although The North British was primarily concerned with the route to Berwick and linking with The Great Northern it persisted with the route south of Hawick towards Carlisle despite blocking tactics from the Caledonian. It constructed, through a subsidiary company called The Border Union Railway, a route into Carlisle opening on 1 June 1862, the total length being $98\frac{1}{4}$ miles from Edinburgh.

The North British also took over the Port Carlisle Railway (which allowed a route into Carlisle that avoided the irritated Caledonian, who had purchased land in the way of the North British!) and gained a line to the port of Silloth. The 13-mile Silloth Bay & Docks Company line gave the North British a port and therefore freight business via ships from eastern Scotland to Ireland and Liverpool. The arrival of the Midland Railway into Carlisle from Leeds in 1876 allowed through running from London St Pancras to Edinburgh via the Midlands and Yorkshire. The LNWR and the Caledonian, who dominated the west coast Anglo/Scottish business, were not keen on the North British gaining access to Carlisle as they saw trains from St Pancras via Settle and the Waverley route, as a threat to their markets. However in reality the Waverley/Settle routes were not competitive in length of journey when compared to the west coast.

As well as the Waverley route main line, this book also covers branches that were operated by the North British Railway. These included Riddings Junction to Langholm, Riccarton Junction to Hexham (the Border Counties line with branches to Rothbury and Morpeth) St Boswells to Roxburgh, Kelso and Tweedmouth, St Boswells to Reston, Galashiels to Selkirk and Galashiels to Edinburgh via Peebles which joined the Waverley route back at Hardengreen Junction. Unfortunately the Lauder branch from Fountainhall has proved elusive in photographic terms on this occasion!

The Waverley route passed through some of the most spectacular scenery in the British Isles. It also had some of the fiercest gradients often situated on curves and was in parts at high altitudes, thus attracting bad weather. Leaving Edinburgh Waverley the route to Portobello East ran through the closed stations of Abbeyhill and Piershill. The North British spur to the important dock areas of Leith and Granton diverged with St Margarets shed by the triangle of junctions. At Portobello East Junction the line branched off from the Berwick route and on through Niddrie North and South Junctions, (that connected to

Gradient Profile of the Waverley Route

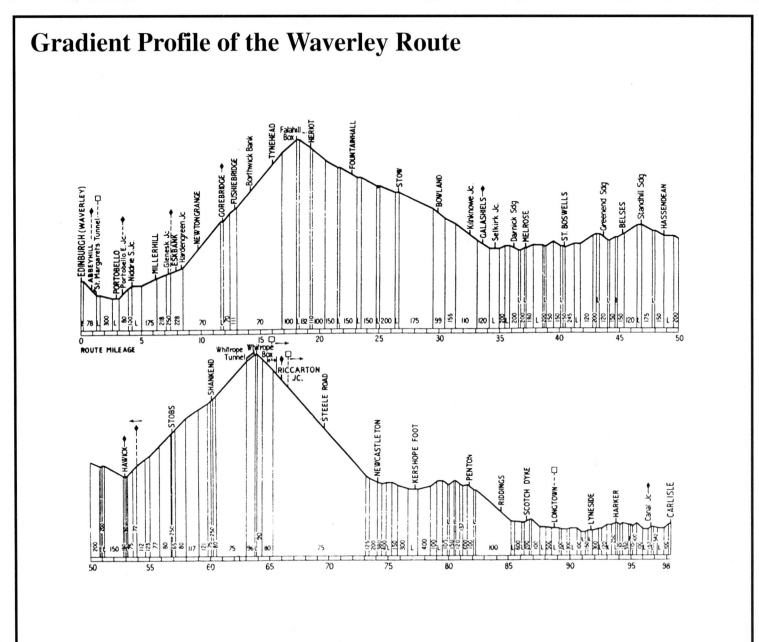

the Edinburgh Circle), and onto Millerhill and its yards. Millerhill Yards were significant in the operation of the Waverley being the source of freight traffic to Carlisle Kingmoor and vice-versa. From Millerhill the climb to Falahill Box, some 18 miles away and mostly at 1 in 70, began. The line was now firmly in the Lothian coalfield and in particular traffic came from Bilston Glen colliery which sent trains via Millerhill to Cockenzie Power Station on the coast. Just after Millerhill came the branch to Dalkeith then Dalkeith and Eskbank before Hardengreen Junction where a long loop line to Peebles branched off, eventually rejoining the Waverley route at Kilnknowe Junction north of Galashiels. On the climb up to the summit came Eskbank, Newtongrange, spurs to Arniston and Lady Victoria pits, Gorebridge, Fushiebridge, (a wartime closure), and Tynehead. Back at Hardengreen Junction there was a small depot for the Falahill bankers and the Peebles locomotives. Between Tynehead and Fushiebridge was Borthwick bank the 1 in 70 here being even fiercer due to the sharp curvature of the line. Falahill summit was 880ft above sea level and once over the top came a long decent to Heriot 79 miles from Carlisle. Next came Fountainhall, the junction for Lauder which closed to passengers in September 1932 but remained open for freight until the end of September 1958. Southwards, still descending down the virtually continuous 1 in 150 grade came Stow, Bowland and Kilnknowe Junction, (where the Peebles loop connected back in), and into Galashiels. Galashiels was a subshed of St Margarets Depot (64A) and was a major coal and water stop with a possible crew change.

South from Galashiels came the branch to Selkirk, (Selkirk Junction), then Melrose, (firstly crossing the 278ft long Redbridge viaduct), 61 miles from Carlisle. Next came St Boswells after Newstead, (closed October 1852), where just to the north came Ravenswood Junction where the line to Reston via Duns branched off. This line was severed from Duns westward in August 1948 after severe flooding washed away the track bed. However, the Duns to Reston passenger service continued until 1951 and freight until 1966. St Boswells had its own locomotive shed for the branches, supplied by Hawick, (64G). St Boswells was also the junction for the line to Roxburgh, Kelso and Tweedmouth (trains ran onto Berwick), which joined to the south at Kelso Junction. A branch also ran to Jedburgh from Roxburgh. The next main stop was Hawick, but first New Belses and Hassendean were passed. Hawick is the largest of the border towns and as a natural turn back for local services from either Edinburgh or Carlisle had an engine shed, (64G), complete with all facilities. Snow ploughs were also based here. From Hawick came another fierce climb of just over 10 miles to Whitrope Summit complete with its lonely signal box. Passing through Stobs and Shankend the line climbed at 1 in 75/80 with Stobs viaduct and the more impressive 15 arch Shankend viaduct being crossed. A tunnel under Sandy Edge, 1,208yds, was negotiated just before the summit at 1,006ft above sea level. Then descending just as sharply at 1 in 75/80 came one of the most remote stations and junctions in the British Isles, Riccarton Junction. Reached only by the railway until 1963, Riccarton was the junction for the wonderful Border Counties line, (closed to passengers in October 1956, freight in 1963), through Kielder Forest to Hexham. The actual service ran from Hawick to Hexham but some trains travelled through to Newcastle. At Reedsmouth Junction the line to Morpeth via Scotsgap branched off with a subsequent branch from there to Rothbury. At Riccarton a small shed was provided for the Whitrope bankers. Continuing the decent, desolate Steele Road was followed by Hermitage or Sandholm viaduct and then Newcastleton where the line levelled out and ran through Kershope Foot after crossing the English border. Following Liddel Water, the line passed through Penton and then into Riddings Junction for the Esk Valley branch to Langholm which diverged north. Closed on 18 September 1964 this line was 7 miles long and operated for just over 100 years. Continuing through Scotch Dyke to Longtown a 3-mile branch to Gretna South Junction diverged to allow freight traffic access to the Glasgow & South Western. Running rights were originally allowed by the Caledonian over a short stretch of their line. Two smaller stations at Lyneside, (closed 1929), and Harker, (also closed 1929 but used in the war), then followed as well as the small Parkhouse Halt which served the RAF depot. The line then crossed over the Caledonian main line from Carlisle to Glasgow by Kingmoor sheds and on to Carlisle No 4 box at Citadel Station via Canal Junction (for Silloth) and Port Carlisle Branch Junction, 98¼ miles from Waverley.

The main motive power depots were situated at each end of the line. Carlisle Canal Shed was initially London Midland following nationalisation but by 1958 moved to the Scottish Region, (68E). By June 1963, (it was back in the LMR coded 12C), it closed moving motive power to Kingmoor. Hawick was

64G with subsheds at Kelso, Riccarton, and St Boswells. Galashiels and Hardengreen Junction were subsheds of the other main depot at Edinburgh St Margarets, (64A), but Haymarket, (64B), also provided the main Pacific power.

In the late 1950s/1960s not surprisingly the traditional NBR and LNER locomotives were gradually replaced by Standard locomotives and diesels. The main express passenger services were the St Pancras to Glasgow 'Waverley' and the St Pancras to Glasgow night sleeper — both travelling via Settle. Services also ran from Edinburgh to Leeds. These services were worked by 'A3s', 'A2s', and occasionally 'V2s'. Local services to and from Hawick were again worked by 'A3s' and 'V2s' but 'B1s' and 'D49s' made regular appearances as well. 'A4s' also visited the route usually covering a failure. Military specials and diversions were totally unpredictable and were pulled by a mixture of Scottish, NER or LMR power. Rail tours were frequent, notably No 4472 *Flying Scotsman* which hauled a Waterloo to Aberdeen train with Southern stock on 25 June 1966. 'V2' No 60836 hauled the 'Granite City Rail Tour' on 3 September 1966, (the day the Great Central closed), which ran from Euston to Aberdeen. 'A4' Pacifics were also regular visitors on rail tours as were 'A2s'. Notable performers were No 60532 *Blue Peter*, which had an Edinburgh to Carlisle service on 8 October 1966 , No 60528 *Tudor Minstrel* which hauled a Manchester to Edinburgh train on 23 April 1966, as well as excursions hauled by 'A4s' Nos 60019 *Bittern* and 60031 *Golden Plover*. The branches were the home of traditional LNER types but standard 2-6-0s were latterly drafted in as replacements. 'Britannias' and Standard Class 4 tanks also became common on the main line as they were displaced by dieselisation in other areas. Diesels to make their mark on the route were 'Peaks' (Class 45), English Electric Type 4s (Class 40s), BRCW Sulzer Bo-Bo Type 2s (Class 26 and 27), Brush Type 4s (Class 47), Claytons (Class 17), and BR Sulzer Class 24s.

Freight services were dominated by the transfer trains from the modernisation plan yards of Millerhill and Kingmoor. Many fitted freights ran daily usually pulled by 'A2s', 'A3s', 'B1s', 'K3s', and 'V2s' with LMR types such as Black 5s, Crabs, 'Jubilees', 'Scots' and 'Patriots' as well as the emerging diesels mentioned above. However, despite the influx of diesels, 'A3s' and 'V2s' did continue to operate freight services working from St Margarets depot well into 1966, No 60052 *Prince Palatine* being the last active 'A3' Pacific. The Ford car trains from Ditton Junction (Halewood), to Edinburgh Bathgate were fascinating sights, especially with two steam locomotives on the front! Local freight services continued on the branches after closure to passengers — most of these dates are mentioned earlier in this introduction or in the captions. At the Edinburgh end of the line, the Lothian coalfield also produced much freight business through the newly extended Millerhill transfer yards.

The last weekend of services was 4/5 January 1969. BR had run a special called 'Farewell to the Waverley' on the 4th hauled by Class 47 No D1947. Another special also ran, organised by the Border Union Railway Society. All were witnessed by flag-waving protesters. A 'Deltic' hauled 11 coach special, the 'Waverley', utilising No D9002 *The King's Own Yorkshire Light Infantry*, ran from Newcastle to Carlisle and then over the Waverley route to Edinburgh, returning home via Berwick. The last freights to pass over the line were the 08.30 Carlisle to Millerhill and a train of empty carflats, the 09.55 Bathgate-Kings Norton. On the Sunday there was a last day special hauled by 'Deltic' locomotive No D9007 *Pinza*, which had an RCTS train from Carlisle to Edinburgh. 'Peak' No D60, *Lytham St Annes*, had the last 'Night Midlander' from Edinburgh to Carlisle and London St Pancras. Trouble was expected and as well as the earlier mentioned incident at Newcastleton, at Hawick a set of points were found to have been tampered with. As a result Class 17 No D8506 was sent ahead to prove the route to Carlisle. Space does not permit me to go into greater detail but Waverley enthusiasts will find, *Waverley, Portrait of a Famous Route* by Roger Siviter, published by Kingfisher, and Neil Caplan's *The Waverley Route*, published by Ian Allan, required reading.

And so the Waverley route passes into history. It carried millions of tons of freight and parcels and millions of passengers. What has happened to them all? Have they transferred to different modes of transport, does the freight traffic now go by road or other rail routes? Could the Waverley or part of it have survived had it lived on into the same era as the Settle to Carlisle?.................Probably.

Special thanks are due to Wendy Chapman and Ron White for their help in producing this book.

Robert Robotham
Charlbury April 1995.

Edinburgh Waverley to Galashiels

Carlisle Canal based 'A3' Pacific No 60068 *Sir Visto* pulls away from Edinburgh Waverley with an express for Carlisle and Leeds in April 1954. No 60068 is starting the 98¼-mile journey where it would be changed for other power to work the train southwards. The run south started along the North British main line to Berwick, diverging from the East Coast route at Portobello East Junction.
Colour Rail (SC372)

Class A3 No 60093 *Coronach*, of Carlisle Canal shed pulls out of Edinburgh Waverley in June 1956 with an express service to Carlisle and Leeds. This train would travel over both the Waverley route and the Settle and Carlisle — what a Mecca that would be today for steam enthusiasts.
J. G. Wallace/ColourRail (SC427)

LNER Class D49/1 4-4-0 No 62712 *Morayshire* is seen near Millerhill with the 16.10 Edinburgh Waverley to Hawick local in May 1960. In the background the Firth of Forth can clearly be seen, the source of much traffic for the North British from docks at Leith and Granton. Millerhill yard acted as a collection point for general freight traffic from eastern Scotland as well as automotive products and coal from the Lothian coalfield.
G. M. Staddon/Colour Rail (SC732)

Left: From Glenesk Junction a short branch line to Dalkeith ran, the main Waverley route station being at Eskbank and Dalkeith. Here 'V3' 2-6-2T No 67668 is seen on a special in the sidings at Dalkeith which had remained open for goods traffic. The date is 25 August 1962.
Colour Rail

The Peebles Loop

Below: 'J37' No 64587, introduced in 1914, stands at Rosewell and Hawthornden on the Peebles loop with a special on 3 February 1962. The complete loop was closed two days later. It had opened from Eskbank to Peebles in July 1855, extending to Galashiels in 1864.
Colour Rail

Left: No 64587 is seen on the same special at Rosslynlee a few miles further to the south. The 'J37' was a superheated development of the 'J35'. Peebles was the main station on the loop where a Caledonian branch from Symington joined. At Leadburn there was also a link to Carstairs.
Colour Rail

Above: It was on the Peebles loop that Scotland's first regular DMU service began and they rapidly replaced steam. Innerleithen was situated on the loop and here a DMU working stands in the neat station with a service from Galashiels to Edinburgh 1961. The snow laden hills add to a most pleasant scene. The line joined back on the Waverley route proper at Kilnknowe Junction. The loop was formally closed on the 5 February 1962 after No 64587's performance on the 3rd. Today, Peebles has no railways.
Colour Rail

Left: Standard Class 4MT 2-6-0, No 76111 climbs up through Tynehead to Falahill with the Parly local service from Edinburgh to Hawick in 1959. No 76111 was a Thornton locomotive borrowed for this particular working. Standard locomotives were becoming more regular performers by this date, replacing the traditional North British and LNER types. *Colour Rail*

Right: 'Peak' diesels were regular performers on the Waverley route and No D24 is seen passing through Tynehead station on 2 September 1965 with the lines' most famous service, the 'Waverley' which ran from Edinburgh Waverley to St. Pancras via Leeds. D24 has the up service and is tackling the climb to Falahill summit. Still two miles to go at 1 in 70. *J. Spencer Gilks collection/Colour Rail*

Left: 'B1' 4-6-0 No 61350 seems to have a good head of steam despite the climb to Falahill with the 16.10 Edinburgh. Waverley to Hawick in July 1963. Based at St Margarets until April 1966, No 61350 was withdrawn from Dunfermline in November 1966. *K. M. Falconer/Colour Rail (SC882)*

Left: On the climb from Hardengreen Junction up to Falahill, which was mostly at 1 in 70, came Borthwick bank. English Electric Type 4, (Class 40), No D251 climbs up to the summit with a fitted freight from Millerhill to Carlisle on the 2 September 1965.
J. Spencer Gilks collection/Colour Rail

Below: Near the summit of Borthwick bank at Falahill. 'A3' Pacific No 60041 *Salmon Trout* is seen with the 09.50 (SO) Edinburgh to Leeds via Carlisle on 3 July 1965. The locomotive is complete with German style smoke deflectors, double chimney and yellow stripe on the cab side which barred it working south of Carlisle on the LNWR main line. The sidings at the summit are seen to the right of the locomotive.
Colour Rail

Left: 'B1' No 61354 is seen skirting Gala water at Fountainhall with a local from Hawick to Edinburgh Waverley in September 1965. No 61354 was allocated to St Margarets/Galashiels depot and the train and locomotive look in smart condition. At Fountainhall was the junction for Lauder, a 12-mile line that closed to passengers on 12 September 1932. Freight continued until 1 October 1958, the last special running on the 15 November of the same year.
J. Spencer Gilks collection/Colour Rail (SC730)

Above: 'V2' No 60813, with small smoke deflectors, races along in fine style near Stow with another down fitted freight service on 14 July 1965.The Waverley route freight services were dominated by these fast transfer trains between Millerhill and Kingmoor.
Colour Rail

Above: 'A3' No 60095 *Flamingo* in original condition leaves Galashiels in June 1950 with an Edinburgh local service. The train is passing Kilnknowe Junction, where the line to Peebles branched off; closing on 5 February 1962.
J. R. Smith/Colour Rail (SC865)

Right: 'A3' No 60093 *Coronach* arrives at Galashiels with an up local to Carlisle in June 1957. The 'A3' is in as built condition and the blood and custard stock are fine examples of Gresley coaches. This photograph makes a good contrast with that of No D5316 on the rear cover.
The late A. G. Cramp/Colour Rail (SC591)

Above: 'A4' No 60031 *Golden Plover* stands at Galashiels with an up special on 18 April 1965. The locomotive shed at Galashiels is situated on the up side to the locomotive's left hand side. No 60031 has acquired the yellow stripe limiting it from working south of Crewe on the newly electrified LNWR main line.

22   *G. Devine/Colour Rail (SC594)*

Right: On shed at Galashiels, (a subshed of St Margarets coded 64A), 'D34' 4-4-0 No 62484 *Glen Lyon* is seen in May 1959. No 62484 was the last surviving North British 'Glen' locomotive. They were common performers on the Peebles loop until gradually replaced by Standard steam locomotives and diesels.
D. H. Beecroft/Colour Rail (SC389)

'A4' Pacific No 60027 *Merlin* of Haymarket shed stands at 'Galashiels, Change for Innerleithen and Peebles', with a local for Carlisle on 31 March 1961. The 'A4s' were often used as substitute power for the failure of more regular locomotives. Galashiels was also the junction for Selkirk, a line which ran through Abbotsford Ferry and Lindean from Selkirk Junction, having closed to passengers on 10 September 1951. Across the river from Abbotsford Ferry station was Abbotsford House, the home of Sir Walter Scott. The line closed to freight on 2 November 1964.
GTR Slides (1248)

Galashiels to Riccarton Junction

Melrose station, (which regularly won awards for its flower beds!), is seen on 31 March 1961 with 'B1' No 61108 of St Margarets/ Galashiels arriving on the 16.10 local service from Edinburgh Waverley to Hawick. The ruins of the Melrose Abbey lay next to the station and an original North British lamp standard can be seen next to the locomotive.
GTR Slides (1305)

Below: Standard '2MT' No 78047 stands at St Boswells with the branch train to Kelso and Berwick on 6 March 1963. This train passed through Roxburgh where the line to Jedburgh branched off. The standard locomotives were steadily displacing the more traditional NBR types by this date.
Colour Rail

Right: North of St Boswells station was the junction at Ravenswood for Duns and Reston. Bad flooding on 12 August 1948 caused much damage to the route which caused it to be closed from Duns westwards. The Reston to Duns portion remained open for passengers until 1951 and for goods until 1966. However, by 27 September 1948 passenger services were withdrawn from St Boswells to Greenlaw, and the track was lifted between Greenlaw and Duns. On 4 April 1959 'Glen' 4-4-0 No 62471 *Glen Falloch* is seen with the 'Scott Country Rail Tour', a Branch Line Society train. Here the special is seen on the Reston line at Earlston.
Colour Rail

Later in the day, 4 April 1959, 'Glen' 4-4-0 No 62471 *Glen Falloch*
is seen with the 'Scott Country Rail Tour', a Branch Line Society
train at Gordon, which at the time remained open for goods services
until closing in July 1965.
Colour Rail

The trip ended at Greenlaw, (the rest of the line having been flood-damaged to Duns), and here No 62471 and her immaculate coaches make a marvellous study. No 62471 was shedded at St Margarets/Galashiels.
Colour Rail

Above left: Standard '3MT' No 77004 shunts at Duns with the pick up freight to Berwick in March 1966. Passenger services ceased in 1951 and 1966 was the last year for freight.
J. Spencer Gilks collection/Colour Rail (SC720)

Below left: 'B1' No 61324 is seen at Duns on 14 April 1963. The train was an SLS/BLS special, the 'Scottish Rambler' which toured the Kelso line as well as the stub from Reston to Duns on the same day.
Colour Rail

Below: No 61324 is seen at Chirnside on the same day with the SLS/BLS special. Chirnside was situated between Duns and Reston.
Colour Rail (SC871)

St Boswells to Roxburgh and Kelso

Left: Standard '2MT' 2-6-0 No 78048 is seen on the 11.30 St Boswells to Kelso, a half-mile east of Roxburgh at Heiton Siding on 30 May 1962. One coach seemed to be sufficient for the traffic requirements at the time. From Roxburgh was a short Branch to Jedburgh. A 7-mile line, it opened in July 1856, passenger services being suspended following the August 1948 flooding. It closed to freight in August 1964.
Mike Mensing

Below: Kelso had a fairly substantial station and here, Standard 2MT No 78047 waits to leave with the 4.00pm St Boswells to Berwick service on 30 May 1962. No 78048 had the last return passenger working on 13 June 1964, freight traffic between Kelso and Tweedmouth ceasing in March 1968.
Mike Mensing

34

Left: Ivatt '2MT' 2-6-0 No 46479 is seen on the 1.50pm Tweedmouth to St Boswells freight restarting from Kelso on 30 May 1962. Livestock, coal and agricultural traffic was the day to day business. After Kelso came Coldstream where another branch through Wooler linked back to the East Coast route at Alnmouth. This line proved invaluable as a diversionary route during the 1948 floods.
Mike Mensing

Galashiels to Riccarton Junction (cont)

Right: 'A1' Pacific No 60152 *Holyrood* storms away from St Boswells with an express for Carlisle and Leeds on a freezing sunny morning in January 1962. No 60152 was a Haymarket locomotive which provided the more 'up market' locomotives from the northern end of the line, leaving St Margarets to provide the 'V2s' and 'B1s'.
The late David Hepburn-Scott/Colour Rail (SC364)

Class 24 No D5116 stands at Hawick station on an Edinburgh
Waverley service, the 09.20 from Carlisle in August 1968. Note the
tall signal box which gave a panoramic view of the station and
yards.

R. B. McCartney/Colour Rail (DE1061)

'A3' No 60068 *Sir Visto* looks very smart as it waits for the off at
Hawick with an Edinburgh train on 15 August 1961. The driver
looks back and the locomotive has been watered for the long climb
through St Boswells to Falahill.
Colour Rail

Left: 'D49/1' No 62715 *Roxburghshire*, is shunted in Hawick shed yard by Standard 2MT 2-6-0, No 78046 in May 1959. Hawick shed was coded 64G and had subsheds at Riccarton Junction and St Boswells.
J. Beecroft/Colour Rail (SC392)

Above: Clayton Class 17 No D8606 leaves Hawick shed with a brake van in June 1967. The Claytons were common performers on the Waverley route but were withdrawn relatively quickly by BR. Note the recess for the tablet catcher in the cabside and the new application of corporate blue livery.
Colour Rail

Left: 'Peak' diesel No D14 stands at Hawick with the 14.45 Edinburgh to Carlisle in June 1968. Mail is being loaded into the brake and the driver awaits the right of way for the climb to Whitrope which began at 1 in 75 just south of the station.
R. B. McCartney/Colour Rail (DE1010)

Right: 'J39' 0-6-0 No 64733 gets away from Hawick with a pick up freight for Carlisle, its home depot, in September 1959. The 'J39s' were equally at home on passenger or freight work being regular performers on the branch to Langholm.
Colour Rail (SC822)

Above: Unlike most of the Waverley route stations, Stobs station was relatively sheltered and here 'V2' No 60969 runs down the bank towards Hawick with a Millerhill freight in July 1962.
J. Spencer Gilks collection/Colour Rail (SC740)

Right: Approaching Shankend station, 'A1' No 60159 *Bonnie Dundee* has a local for Carlisle in June 1961. Note the neat embankments and general condition of the permanent way which are a credit to the gangers.
The late Malcolm Thompson/Colour Rail (SC856)

43

Above: 'A2/3' No 60519 *Honeyway* runs through Shankend station with a down fitted freight and parcels service to Edinburgh in June 1961. No 60519 was a Haymarket locomotive and is in a rather grubby state as is her stable mate No 60159 in the previous photograph.

Right: Shankend had a few sidings for local freight requirements and here, No 78047 is seen on a pick up working from Hawick to Carlisle on 4 September 1965. The sidings were lifted towards the end of the lines' operation as this local traffic gradually ceased on a national scale.

Colour Rail

The late Malcolm Thompson/Colour Rail (SC857)

Left: The car trains to and from Bathgate were regular business on the Waverley route Here 'B1' No 61407 and 'Patriot' No 45530 *Sir Frank Ree* head a train to Cowley over Shankend Viaduct. The station is just ahead and the date is July 1963.
J. Spencer Gilks collection/Colour Rail (SC731)

Right: 'A2' No 60534, *Irish Elegance* storms over Whitrope summit with an Edinburgh to Leeds service in May 1961. The 'A2' is going well with nine on and will now descend at 1 in 90/1 in 75 towards Riccarton and Newcastleton. The bridge is the B6399 crossing the road from Newcastleton to Hawick.
The late Malcolm Thompson/ Colour Rail (SC859)

Standard '4MT' No 76050 climbs up to the summit with a Carlisle to Hawick local service on 16 July 1965. These shots of Whitrope show the remoteness of the surrounding country the Waverley route passed through, often covered in snow.
Colour Rail

On the 4 September 1965 'B1' No 61347 pulls up to the summit on a Kingmoor to Millerhill unfitted freight. No 61347 was allocated to Dalry Road at this date, transferring to St Margarets the following month and finally to Thornton Junction, prior to withdrawal in April 1967. *Colour Rail*

No 61347's fireman fills another shovelful of coal as the summit is approached. The regulator is fully open as the end of the 1 in 75/90 is reached. Once past the summit came Whitrope Tunnel, the descent towards Hawick and some rest for the fireman!
Colour Rail

Left: Smart 'V2' No 60836 hauled the 'Granite City' rail tour on 3 September 1966 from Euston to Aberdeen. Here she storms towards the summit at Whitrope with a train of mixed stock — including new Mark II coaches. *The late A. E. R. Cope/Colour Rail*

Right: Approaching the summit 'A4' No 60027 *Merlin* is working hard with an Edinburgh bound special train on 5 June 1965. The 'A4' is in work-stained condition but has a fine exhaust and appears to have little problem with its heavy load. This train was a Scottish Locomotive Preservation Fund train which ran from Edinburgh to Newcastle then on to Carlisle and Edinburgh via the Waverley route. 'A3' No 60052 *Prince Palatine* had hauled the train from Edinburgh but had failed with a hot box at Carlisle. Luckily, No 60027 was available as an able substitute. *Colour Rail*

'V2' No 60970 brews up at Riccarton in preparation for the climb up to Whitrope from Newcastleton, with her fitted freight service for Millerhill. Riccarton Junction was often used as a place for a blow up and for recessing freights if required. *G. Parry collection/Colour Rail (SC 330)*

51

'A4' No 60027 *Merlin* stands at Riccarton Junction with the special train seen on page 50 on 5 June 1965. The locomotive is filthy, being a last minute substitute for 'A3' No 60052 *Prince Palatine*. *J. G. Wallace/Colour Rail (SC537)*

The last northbound special to run over the Waverley route was an RCTS special from Leeds on Sunday 5 January 1969. The train was hauled by 'Deltic' No D9007 *Pinza* and is seen (in immaculate condition), at Riccarton Junction.
The late Alan Watts/Colour Rail (DE1572)

'A4' No 60031 *Golden Plover*, on a southbound special, gets away from Riccarton Junction for Carlisle on 18 April 1965. The high view point shows the Border Counties line to Reedsmouth and Hexham running away to the east.
The late A. E. R. Cope/Colour Rail (SC207)

Riccarton Junction to Morpeth and Hexham

'K3' 2-6-0 No 61897 takes a train over Kielder Forest viaduct with a smart Thompson coach in tow in the summer of 1953. The teetering footbridge over the river looks somewhat suspect. After the closure of the line to freight on 1 September 1958, passenger services having ceased on 15 October 1956, the viaduct was preserved, but is now submerged under the Kielder Forest reservoir. The line's passenger service was sparse, there being three return services from Hawick to Newcastle via Riccarton Junction on week days.
Colour Rail (BRE733)

Above: 'D49/2' No 62771 *The Rufford* leaves Reedsmouth Junction with a service from Hawick to Hexham and Newcastle in the summer of 1953. The line forking to the right runs through Scotsgap to Morpeth, and No 62771 has just come off the Kielder line, which had opened on 1 July 1862.
Colour Rail (BRE719)

Right: 'D30' 4-4-0 No 62435 *Norna* is seen near Chollerton with a local service from Hexham to Riccarton in Summer 1953. No 62435 survived in traffic until December 1957, being scrapped at Inverurie works the same month.
Colour Rail (BRE211)

Left: 'D30/2' 4-4-0 No 62423 *Dugald Dalgetty* calls at Humshaugh on a service from Hexham to Hawick in 1953. No 62423 was introduced in 1914, a development of the famous Reid Scott class like No 62435 in the previous photograph. Note the bee-hives by the locomotive.
Colour Rail (BRE716)

Below: The Border Counties line joined the Newcastle to Carlisle line at Hexham. 'J21' No 65033 runs over the Tyne bridge onto the main line with a Gresley coach on a service from Reedsmouth in 1953.
Colour Rail (BRE218)

Left: 'J27' No 65842 stands at Woodburn, between Reedsmouth and Morpeth, on the Thursdays only freight service from Morpeth in September 1966.
J. M. Boyes/Colour Rail (BRE222)

Above: From Scotsgap a branch to Rothbury ran opening on 19 October 1870. Some 13 miles long, it served not only the local communities but also various limestone quarries. Passenger services ceased from 15 September 1952, but freight continued until 11 November 1966. At Long Witton 'J25' No 65727, fitted with a small snow-plough, heads for Rothbury in 1953.
Colour Rail (BRE221)

Below: A car park now stands on the site of Rothbury station, but in 1952, 'J21' No 65110 prepares to return to Scotsgap with a rather lengthy train. Note the turntable and tiny locomotive shed. There were three trains a day for most of the line's existence but specials did run for the Rothbury spring race meetings on an 'as required' basis. *Colour Rail (BRE220)*

Right: 'K3' No 61934 heads a Kingmoor to Millerhill fitted freight up to Steele Road in June 1961. At this time No 61934 was allocated to Berwick, moving to Ardsley later in the year.
The late Malcolm Thompson/Colour Rail (SC879)

Riccarton Junction to Carlisle

'Above: 'A3' No 60093 *Coronach* heads the down 'Waverley'
express, complete with headboard, at Steele Road in June 1961. The
locomotive is in very smart condition and will be coasting down the
1 in 75 towards Newcastleton. The down 'Waverley' left St Pancras
at 09.15 arriving at Edinburgh at 18.34. It was allowed 1hr 36min
for the Waverley route portion of the journey.

The late Malcolm Thompson/Colour Rail (SC864)

Above: 'B1' No 61294 approaches the station at Steele Road with a northbound freight in June 1964. No 61294 has a fine clear exhaust as she climbs up to Whitrope summit, some five miles distant.
J. B. Snell/Colour Rail

Right: A classic study of two Class 17 Clayton diesels descending through Steele Road with a Millerhill to Kingmoor freight on 3 September 1965. A gradient post can be seen in the foreground indicating the descent to Newcastleton as Nos D8606 and D8601 coast down the grade. The Claytons had two Paxman 450bhp power units.
The late Derek Cross/Colour Rail

Left: Hermitage or Sandholm viaduct was situated just north of Newcastleton and 'B1' No 61294 crosses it with a down freight in June 1964. The locomotive is in filthy condition, but thankfully someone has cleaned the numbers!
J. B. Snell/Colour Rail (SC596)

Above: No 61294 is seen climbing away from Newcastleton towards Sandholm viaduct with the same train as seen in the previous shot. No 61294 was transferred to St Margarets shed in June 1964, so this is an early working for the locomotive over the Waverley.
J. B. Snell/Colour Rail

'J39' No 64888 stands in Riddings Junction with the Langholm branch train in May 1959. It was here that the symbolic lifting of a section of track took place on 6 January 1969 to formally truncate the line.
The late D. H. Beecroft/Colour Rail (SC398)

'A3' No 60093 *Coronach* stands at Riddings Junction with a stopper for Edinburgh Waverley in May 1959. The 'A3' is in magnificent condition and makes the connection for the Langholm branch, as seen in the previous photograph.
The late D. H. Beecroft/Colour Rail (SC376)

Ex-LMS '4MT' 2-6-0 No 43139 returns to Riddings Junction from
Langholm with the branch freight for Carlisle on 31 March 1961.
The Class 4MTs were displacing the more traditional 'J39s' by this
stage.

Right: Ivatt '4MT' No 43023 waits at Langholm with the branch train to Riddings Junction in summer 1963. The passenger service survived until 15 June 1964. The line ran through the delightful Esk Valley, and crossed Liddel Water on a fine viaduct once it had diverged from the Waverley route to the North of Riddings Junction. Langholm trains arrived in the up bay platform at Riddings Junction and then ran round before propelling back into the down bay. *F. W. Shuttleworth/Colour Rail (SC852)*

Left: On 10 October 1963 No 43011 was in charge of the 3.28pm service to Carlisle. Allocated to Carlisle Kingmoor at this time, No 43011 was to survive in service until February 1967. *Hugh Ballantyne*

Below: Class A2 Pacific No 60537 *Bachelors Button* arrives at Riddings Junction with the 13.28 Carlisle to Edinburgh Waverley on 31 March 1961. Allocated to Haymarket, 64B, No 60537 survived in traffic until December 1962.
GTR Slides (1160)

Right: Ivatt Class 4MT No 43121 is seen at Longtown on an LCGB special on 14 October 1967. No 43121 was allocated to Carlisle Kingmoor, 12A, to work local services and branch pick-up freights. South of Longtown was the junction to Gretna, which allowed The North British access to the Glasgow & South Western via a short section of the Caledonian.
Colour Rail

Above: Peppercorn Class A2 No 60532 *Blue Peter* is turned at Carlisle Kingmoor on 8 October 1966. The locomotive had just hauled a special from Edinburgh to Carlisle and is in superb condition.

The late E. R. Cope/Colour Rail (SC588)

Right: Carlisle Canal shed was closed on 19 June 1963. It was the southern home of the Waverley route's locomotives and the most famous of these were perhaps its fleet of 'A3' Pacifics. These were notably, No 60068 *Sir Visto*, 60079 *Bayardo*, 60093 *Coronach*, and 60095 *Flamingo*. This photograph shows No 60093 and the cab of No 60079 on shed at Canal in Summer 1959.

Colour Rail

Left: D49/1 No 62712 *Morayshire*, awaits departure from Carlisle to Hawick with the 18.13 local in 1960. Local services on the Waverley route tended to depart from these bay platforms at the north end of Citadel station as did the local trains to Silloth. The expresses used the main platforms where they changed locomotives. *Colour Rail*

Below: A good overall study of the terminus at Silloth sees Class 26 No D5310 about to depart with the 18.00 service to Carlisle in September 1964. Silloth gave the North British a port which allowed freight from eastern Scotland to travel to the north west via ship. DMUs gradually replaced locomotive hauled trains on the Silloth branch until its closure. *J. Spencer Gilks collection/Colour Rail (DE1444)*

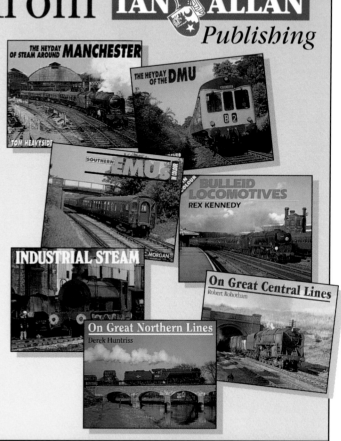